In a Flash

D1132118

Eric Walters

ORCA BOOK PUBLISHERS

Orca currents

Library and Archives Canada Cataloguing in Publication

Walters, Eric, 1957-
In a flash / Eric Walters.

(Orca currents)
ISBN 978-1-55469-035-0 (bound).--ISBN 978-1-55469-034-3 (pbk.)

I. Title. II. Series.

PS8595.A598I5 2008   jC813'.54   C2008-902647-0

Summary: Is an event involving a mob ever a good thing?

First published in the United States, 2008
Library of Congress Control Number: 2008927296

Orca Book Publishers gratefully acknowledges the support for its publishing
programs provided by the following agencies: the Government of Canada
through the Book Publishing Industry Development Program and the
Canada Council for the Arts, and the Province of British Columbia
through the BC Arts Council and the Book Publishing Tax Credit.

Cover design by Teresa Bubela
Cover photography by Dreamstime

Orca Book Publishers
PO Box 5626, Station B
Victoria, BC Canada
V8R 6S4

Orca Book Publishers
PO Box 468
Custer, WA USA
98240-0468

www.orcabook.com
Printed and bound in Canada.
Printed on 100% PCW recycled paper.

12 11 10 09 • 5 4 3 2

Author Note

Technologies like the Internet, Facebook, MSN, cell phones and text messaging aren't just forms of communication but types of raw power. We stand on the verge of a revolution in how they can be used, and I believe this generation of technologically literate people—people primarily under the age of twenty—will discover how to use this power to create social justice, spread information, break the monopolies of power interests and overthrow totalitarian governments. And maybe, have a little fun along the way.

chapter one

"What do you think?" I asked Oswald.

"She's wearing a baseball cap. She could be part of it."

"Lots of people wear baseball caps," Julia said. "That doesn't mean she's part of anything—she might just have *terrible* fashion sense."

"Which reminds me," I said, "where is *your* cap?"

She smirked. "I forgot it...I guess that means that I won't be able to partici—"

I whipped out a cap I had tucked away inside my jacket. The smirk on *her* face was replaced by the smirk on *my* face as I handed it to her.

"I don't know why I have to do this, Ian. How about if I just do the taping instead?"

"Nope. You've been making fun of us for doing this, so you need to take part instead of just watching. Put on the cap."

She took it from me and settled it on her head, trying not to disturb her hair. When had she become so concerned about her hair...and her clothes...and her makeup?

"Wrong way," I said.

"What do you mean?"

"Your birthday is in September," I said.

"Which is an odd month, not an even," Oswald said. "You have to put your cap on backward like mine."

Before she could think or react or speak, I reached over and spun her cap around, deliberately smushing her hair in the process.

"Look, there's three people over there with baseball caps," Oswald said.

"Three is good. Thirty would be better."

The last thing I wanted was to fail. I wanted a crowd, not just to show Julia what it was like when it worked really well, but because I was more than just a participant this time—I was the organizer.

"What time is it?" Julia asked.

I looked at my watch. "It's ten forty-one."

"So it's supposed to start in ten minutes."

"Twelve minutes," I said.

"*Exactly* twelve minutes," Oswald said. "It all starts at the stroke of ten fifty-three."

"Yeah right. You two make it sound like you're planning an armed robbery."

I looked at Oswald. "An armed robbery might take less coordination than this," I said. "We better get into position. Are you going to tape from up here?"

"Perfect spot. Great view of the whole area and far enough away that nobody will even notice me." He looked around. "And some nice escape routes."

Julia suddenly looked uncomfortable. "Escape routes? Why would he need an escape route?"

"We *all* need an escape route," Oswald said.

"You just stay close to me," I said. "Wherever I go, you go. Understand?"

"I understand that I'm not letting you out of my sight, but that doesn't answer my question. Why do we need an escape route?"

"It's just planning. If you fail to plan, you plan to fail."

"Great, you're quoting fortune cookie slogans. Why do we need an escape route?" she repeated.

Persistence was one of her strengths.

"Well, sometimes, somebody might object to what we're going to be doing."

"And who might that somebody be?" she pressed.

"The usual suspects," Oswald said. "You know, security guards, police."

"Police! You didn't mention that we could get arrested?" she snapped, stabbing a finger at me.

"We're not going to get arrested," I said, trying to reassure her. "Nobody ever gets arrested...well, hardly anybody."

"And what exactly does *hardly anybody* mean?"

"It means that we don't know anybody who's been arrested, but I heard about one that went wrong in London last year, and a couple of people were arrested. And I think maybe a few people in Madrid this year."

"And there were, like, twenty arrested last month in Los Angeles," Oswald said.

I wished he hadn't mentioned that one.

"How can twenty people be hardly anybody? Twenty is at least eighteen people more than hardly anybody."

"But that one doesn't even count," I said. "They stuck around and argued with the police. We're not arguing with anybody, and we're not sticking around."

"That's *why* we have escape routes," Oswald said. "It's not like this is our first time."

"Where should I meet when this is over?" I asked.

"Head for Dundas Square and we can approximeet."

"Approximeet?" Julia asked.

"It means we'll meet in that approximate area and hook up by cell phone," I explained.

"You two even have your own special little language now?"

"Not just us," I protested. "Lots of people use that word. There's almost a whole new language."

"And what do you call it, Geek Speak?"

I ignored her taunt.

"Look, more people are starting to drift into the area," Oswald said.

There were at least a dozen kids off to the side and another nine or ten wandering through the bedding section of the store.

"They might not even be involved in this," Julia said.

"Yeah right, teenagers always look at bedding in stores."

"Either way, you two better get going or you'll miss it," Oswald said.

I looked at my watch. We had six minutes to get down the escalator and into position.

I pulled two whistles out of my pocket and handed one to Oswald.

"I'll start things off," I said. "And you finish."

"How many minutes do you want?"

"Three...no, make it four."

"Why not five?" Julia asked.

"The longer it goes on the more chance something might go wrong. You know, police might show up."

She didn't look any happier with the idea than she had before. "How about three minutes?"

"Four," I said. "Four minutes. No more, no less."

Oswald held his wrist close to mine. "Let's synchronize our watches."

Julia shook her head. "You two really have been watching too many spy movies."

We ignored her. "When I blow the whistle, just mark the spot on your watch and then go four minutes."

"Which is exactly how much time you

two have to get down there," Oswald said. "You better get going."

"Come on."

We hurried toward the escalator and started down. As we traveled I pulled on my baseball cap. I aimed the bill forward. I was born in April—an even month.

"Do you really think we should do this?" Julia asked.

"If you're too frightened, you don't have to do it."

"I'm not frightened," she protested. "I just don't get the point of it."

"You will. Just stop complaining."

"How do you even know that anybody is going to show up?" she asked.

"Look around. It's clear that some people have shown up. It's just a question of how many we'll get."

"It still only looks like a few to me."

"You don't know that. You'll see." Actually I was hoping that both of us would see. You could never tell with a flash mob. Some were amazing, fantastic, gigantic. Others were just amazing, fantastic, gigantic flops.

"I don't see them yet," she said as we started across the floor of the store and headed toward the bedding section.

"You won't see them until it starts... that's the way it happens," I explained— again hoping that would be the way it went down today.

"But wouldn't they have arrived already?"

"*We* haven't even arrived yet," I said. "That's the way it works. You have to get in and out at the exact time. If too many people hang around before it starts, it would give security a chance to be there."

"We keep going back to this security and police thing. If I get arrested, I'm going to kill you."

"If you kill me, you *would* get arrested. Murder is a crime. This isn't...well, not really."

We cut through the women's clothing section, and suddenly I was surrounded by racks and racks of colorful lingerie and bras. I felt strange and lowered my eyes. I didn't want Julia to see me staring at them...but I didn't want her to think that I wasn't interested in them...but I didn't want her to think I was *too* interested in them in some sort of strange, cross-dressing, perverted way or—I bumped into a rack and it almost tipped over.

Julia snickered. "You know if you break it, you gotta buy it."

"Funny, really funny," I said. As I steadied the rack, a few bright orange and pink bras fluttered to the floor. I thought about picking them up, but I really didn't want Julia to see me handling bras. Besides, there wasn't time.

"Come on," I said. I pushed past Julia, and she fell in behind me.

Breaking free of the lingerie, we came to the homewares, and off to the side was the bedding section. There were beds and blankets and sheets and duvets and, best of all, bins filled with pillows.

And that wasn't all. There were kids wearing baseball caps standing around in the section—and more coming from all sides, converging on the beds.

"And you thought nobody was going to show up," I said.

I looked at my watch. The second hand was sweeping up toward twelve—twenty seconds to go. I walked over to the bins holding the pillows and stopped.

I started to count. There were at least fifty, no sixty, maybe seventy and more still streaming in. About half had their baseball caps on backward; the rest wore the bill to the front. Perfect. There was almost exactly the same number of people on both teams.

I looked at my watch again. Five seconds. I popped the whistle into my mouth and blew as loud as I could—and then I was smashed in the back of the head.

chapter two

I grabbed a pillow from the bin, turned around and swung it at my attacker—it was a girl. She ducked under my swing, hit me with a second shot and danced away to start swinging at somebody else.

All around me there were dozens and dozens of people engaged in a gigantic free-for-all pillow fight!

"Here, take this," I yelled at Julia as I tossed a pillow to her.

She looked at me and opened her mouth

to say something, but before the words could come out she was hit in the side of the head. She staggered and toppled over, landing on a bed!

I should have cheered—after all, she was on the other side, the backward hats—but I was worried about how she was going to react.

She jumped back to her feet. Her expression quickly went from shocked to angry. Making Julia angry was never wise. She leaped across the bed and started swinging at the person who had hit her.

I came to the defense of the guy she was attacking—after all, he *was* on my team—and hit Julia on the arm, knocking the pillow out of her grip. Before she could retrieve it, she was hit by two other people.

I ran around a display case and started a battle with two guys, catching one with an upper-cut that knocked the baseball cap off his head. He looked surprised, and then he laughed and put his hat back on his head.

Two girls were jumping on a bed and exchanging hits and giggles. Finally one of them jumped off, and the second trailed after her. The two of them took glancing blows from other people as they ran across the department and disappeared into women's wear.

There was playful combat everywhere. I didn't have much time to look around, but there had to be close to a hundred people around me, yelling, laughing and swinging their pillows.

On the edges of the battle other people watched. There were grown-ups holding their kids by the hand or loaded down with shopping bags, looking stunned or amused or confused. Some laughed and pointed, and others hurried away like they were scared. There had to be almost as many people watching as there were participating.

One of the pillows burst and a million white feathers shot into the air like a billowing cloud! The crowd—watching and fighting—erupted into gasps and screams and laughter.

There was a loud whistle blast—Oswald, signaling the end.

I dropped my pillow to the floor as did everybody else. I looked around, trying to find Julia in the crowd, as everybody instantly started to run away, going in every direction, out of the bedding section.

I caught sight of her. "Julia! This way!" I yelled.

Julia ran over, and I grabbed her by the hand as we started running. We slipped between the onlookers, breaking free. I grabbed the hat off her head and took mine off as well. I stuffed them into the inside pocket of my coat. With the hats gone we could blend into the background.

We turned a corner into the women's clothing section, leaving the bedding behind. I stopped running, jerking Julia to a walk beside me.

"What are you doing?" she hissed. "We have to get out of here!"

She tried to start running again, but I held her hand tightly, not letting her go.

"People who run get chased because they're running away from something," I said. "We need to walk. Just walk with me."

I kept hold of her hand.

"Slow down your breathing," I said.

She looked anxiously over her shoulder in the direction we'd run from.

"And stop looking guilty," I said quietly. "Look casual."

"I don't feel so casual."

"Maybe that's the wrong word. Try to relax."

That probably wasn't the right word either.

It felt awkward holding Julia's hand. We'd been friends for a long time, but we'd also gone out on a date—once.

We'd both agreed—halfway through that date—that maybe it was better for us to just stay friends. So, we had become just two friends who'd gone to a movie together once and shared some popcorn. But I still wondered and thought about sharing something else... someday...maybe. There was something about Julia. She was smart and pretty and funny, and in those moments when she wasn't driving me crazy, I'd have thoughts that maybe we could be more than just friends.

"This way," I said as we walked through a door leading out of the store and onto the street.

I turned right and she turned left, and I dragged her in my direction.

"This way," I said.

"But isn't Dundas Square the other way?" she asked.

"It is. We're going to circle around and come at it so we can enter from the side away from the store. Just in case."

"Okay, sure. By the way, I think you can let go of my hand now," Julia said.

"Oh, yeah...of course. I just wasn't thinking."

My hand was all sweaty. I wiped it on my pants, trying to be casual about it.

"Boy, did you take some hits," Julia said.

"*Me?* You were hit so hard you got knocked off your feet!"

"You should have seen the shot I gave him after that," she said and started chuckling.

"I guess the important thing is that you had fun."

"I didn't say that," she said.

"You didn't have fun?"

"Well, it certainly was...what word am I looking for...um...I've got it. The word is *stupid*."

"Are you telling me you didn't enjoy that?"

"Which part was I supposed to enjoy? Being worried about being arrested, or hanging out with a herd of nerds?"

"You're telling me that you didn't enjoy it at all?" I asked, unable to believe my ears.

She shrugged. "It just didn't have any purpose."

"That *is* the purpose," I argued. "A flash mob isn't supposed to have a purpose. It's just something that happens for no apparent reason."

"Well, then you really succeeded with this one because it had no reason."

"The reason is just to have—"

"Ian! Julia!"

Oswald ran toward us, waving his arms, a big smile on his face. He looked like *he* thought it was fun.

"That was outstanding!" he yelled as he gave me a big high five.

"Glad *you* liked it," I said, giving Julia a dirty look.

"I loved it! Wait until you see the video. Let's get something to drink and sit down and watch it."

We went into a little coffee shop just off the square, waiting in line for three hot chocolates, and then we took a table in the corner.

"So what did you think?" Oswald asked Julia.

"She didn't like it," I said before she could answer.

"What didn't you like?" Oswald said.

"Come on, I'm a little old for a pillow fight. I can't believe that you two have been running around the city having pillow fights."

"It's not just pillow fights," I protested.

"Yeah, last week we were part of a flash mob that met on the Main Street subway platform, and we all started clapping," Oswald said.

"Clapping for what?"

"For nothing. If we were clapping for something it wouldn't have been a flash mob," he said.

Julia shook her head sadly. She looked like she pitied us.

"And there was the zombie walk where everybody dressed like a zombie," he said. "And there was the silent disco and—"

"Yeah, they all sound hilarious," Julia said sarcastically.

"Here, look," Oswald said. He turned his camera around so that Julia and I could see the screen.

The camera had a wide-angle lens that showed the whole section of the store from his perch on the second floor.

"How many people do you think were there?" I asked.

"Over a hundred, maybe a hundred and twenty," he said. "That was, without a doubt, the best flash mob I've ever seen."

Julia shook her head slowly. "I can't believe how much work had to go into getting that many nerds together in one place."

"First off, they aren't nerds...well, not all of them," I said. "And second, there's not much work at all. I sent out one e-mail blast, posted it on Facebook and sent a text message fan-out."

"A fan-out?"

"Just like with the campaign against Frankie's," I explained.

Last year I'd used the Internet to create a boycott of the Frankie's restaurant chain. I'd e-mailed forty people, who had e-mailed forty people, who e-mailed forty people, until millions of people saw the e-mail. It had ended up in Frankie's adding healthy choices to their menu. I got on TV, and there were magazine articles written about it—about *me*. For a few weeks I'd been a star.

"This is a lot different than what you did with Frankie's," she said.

"Not really. I used technology to get a bunch of people to do something," I explained.

She shook her head. "With Frankie's you got people to do *something*. Today you got people to do nothing."

"They had a pillow fight," I argued.

"That's what I said. They did *nothing.* They did nothing that meant anything. With all the bad things going on in the world—racism, poverty, wars, hunger—you organized a pillow fight."

"It was a pretty good pillow fight," Oswald argued.

"But it was still a pillow fight." She got up. "I have to go to the washroom."

I watched her walk away.

"It was a *great* pillow fight," Oswald said. "And when I post this online, you'll see that lots of people will be impressed."

"Thanks."

I knew he was right. It had been a great flash mob, and we'd get great postings about it. What did I care if Julia wasn't impressed? But somehow I did.

chapter three

My father was sitting at the dining-room table when I got home. The table was piled with legal papers. He was preparing for a trial. Between him and my mother, who was also a lawyer, there was always a pile of papers lying around somewhere.

He looked up. "So how are you doing?" he asked.

"Great...good...all right, I guess."

He chuckled. "That pretty well covers all options. You sure you're at least all right?"

"Yeah, I guess."

"It's just that you look a little guilty."

"Guilty? What makes you think I'm guilty of anything?"

"If you're a lawyer long enough, you know when somebody's guilty of something. What is it?"

"Nothing. I didn't do anything wrong. Well, I don't think I did."

"Maybe you should tell me about it," he suggested.

"It's nothing."

"Nothing or nothing you want to talk about?"

"Well, maybe a little of both, but I'm really not in trouble. And I don't think I'm doing anything wrong. I don't think."

"Sounds like you need a legal opinion."

"I guess I do."

"I just don't know if you can afford my rates. Good legal advice doesn't come cheap."

"I could always ask Mom," I said.

"You could, but you might have to pay a much higher price," he said.

"Mom won't charge me."

"She won't charge you *money*," he said, "but you'll pay a high price in nagging if she doesn't like what you were doing."

Of course I knew what he meant. Mom was great and everything, but she certainly could hang onto something for a long time. She was like a dog with a bone.

"Well?" my father asked.

"What's your price?"

"A cold Coke, on ice, tall glass."

"Sure, no prob—"

"Three times," he said, holding up three fingers.

"How about twice?"

He reached out his hand and we shook on the deal.

"So what's the problem?" he asked.

I tried to think about where to start. "Do you know what a flash mob is?"

"I don't know about the flash part, but anything to do with mobs doesn't sound very good."

"They're not really mobs. They're just some people," I tried to explain. "Regular people. We agree to meet at a specific place, and we all do the same thing."

"What sort of thing?" he asked, sounding worried.

"It's nothing serious. It's all just fun. It could be that we all clap our hands and cheer for somebody, or we all carry a rose or have on a baseball cap, or maybe carry a musical instrument, or have a pillow fight or everybody dresses like a zombie."

He looked confused. It did sound strange when I tried to describe it. Maybe Julia had a point.

"And we just meet for a few minutes, and then everybody disappears," I added.

"Hold on," he said. "I think I *do* know something about them. I remember reading an article in a magazine. They started in New York, right?"

"Yeah, that's where the first one happened."

"And you've been taking part in these?" he asked.

"Some. I've even organized one."

"Okay. So you're wondering if you're breaking any laws."

"Yeah, that's what I want to know."

"I only know what you've told me, and the little bit I remember from that article," he admitted. "But from what you're saying it sounds like they're pretty harmless."

"That's what I was hoping you'd say. This may sound stupid, but I was afraid we could get charged with something."

"Well, you *could* get charged."

"We could?"

"It would depend on the event or the location," he said. "For example, if you were on private property, you could be charged with trespassing."

"They usually happen in a public place or a store."

"A store isn't public. They might not charge you with trespassing, but they might serve you with notice to bar you from ever going to the store."

"They could do that?"

"Of course they could," he said. "There

are also issues, of course, if anything got damaged."

I thought about the pillow exploding. They wouldn't charge us with that, would they?

"But generally, I think the worst thing that would happen is that you'd be issued a ticket, given a fine."

"I guess that wouldn't be so bad."

"It wouldn't be that bad, but I'd still try to avoid it. The real danger is if something goes wrong."

"What could go wrong?" I asked.

"Lots of things. You put lots of strangers together without a leader and there's always potential for something bad to happen."

"You don't know these people. Flash mobbers are pretty good people."

"I'm sure they are, but you know as well as I do that the unexpected can happen. When you started that campaign against Frankie's, did you think it would ever become that big?"

I shook my head and laughed. "No way. It was just a project for my computer class."

"Who would have thought that you e-mailing forty people and asking them to e-mail forty people, and them e-mailing forty people, would have led to millions of people boycotting the restaurant?"

"Not me," I admitted.

"And did you ever think that you were going to be threatened with a lawsuit?"

I shook my head. Frankie's had quickly become aware of the boycott, traced the e-mails back to me and threatened me with legal action.

"But they didn't actually sue me."

"That's only because you have two trial lawyers for parents. They knew they couldn't bluff you," my father said. "All I'm saying is that you can't always predict where things will go, so be careful."

"I'll be careful," I said. But maybe not careful enough.

chapter four

"Were you online last night?" Oswald asked.

"I was pretty busy," I said. "Lots of homework."

"So, you didn't see all the comments about our flash mob. People loved it!"

"Not everybody," I said.

He grabbed me by the shoulders and spun me around. "Julia is not going to like *anything*," he said. "And believe me, after dating her I have no doubts about that."

The three of us had been friends since kindergarten. Last spring, for three weeks, the two of them had become *boy*friend and *girl*friend. Forget about how bad it had worked out for them, for me it had just about been the worst three weeks of my semi-adult life. It was like a really bad teen movie where nobody lives happily ever after.

"Oswald, just because you were stupid enough to date her doesn't mean I'm stupid enough."

Julia and I had never told him about our half-date—it took place the day after the two of them broke up. We'd both agreed it was better that he knew nothing about it. Julia thought he might have felt betrayed.

I wasn't being that noble.

If I told Oswald I would have to admit that I was equally stupid for trying to turn a friend into a girlfriend. After all the grief I'd given him, he would never let me hear the end of it.

"And, you know, she's getting even harder to deal with," Oswald said.

He was right about that.

"Every since she got elected school president, she's been nearly impossible to be around."

"I hear you," I said. "I didn't think that being made student president would mean you had to stop having a sense of humor," I said.

"I told you not to invite her," he said.

"I know."

"I told you she wouldn't find it funny."

"I know."

"Then why did you do it?" he asked.

I shrugged. "We're still friends...I just wanted to include her."

"You tried. It failed, so don't do it again. She just doesn't understand. She thinks it's pointless."

"Well, most of these flash mobs are pointless," I said.

"And that is the point."

"Yeah, yeah, I understand. How ironic, how cool, how—"

"Stop right now!" Oswald commanded. "Now you're sounding like Julia!" He sounded alarmed.

"I was just thinking," I said, "wouldn't it be just as much fun if we set up a flash mob that actually meant something, that had a point, that—"

The first bell sounded in the distance, signaling ten minutes until we had to be in our first period class.

"We better get going," Oswald said. "It would be *pointless* to be late."

The school was just up ahead. There were two ways to get there—the long way around to the front doors, and the short way, cutting across the bridge. We didn't have time for the long way.

We both made the same turn—toward the bridge—without talking, although I knew we both had the same thought. Sometimes the bridge was fine. Other times there were other kids, older kids who didn't even go to our school, and sometimes they hassled kids. It was usually okay in the morning—I guess punks liked to sleep in.

As we rounded a corner we could see the bridge and the people on it—the punks on it. There were four, no, five of them, sitting on the railings of the narrow footbridge that crossed the creek.

"Too late to go back," Oswald said. "Maybe they'll leave us alone."

"Yeah, I guess that could happen," I agreed.

Up ahead three girls—they looked like little niners—were walking across. The punks were hooting and hollering at them.

"Look, there's a man coming from the other direction," Oswald said.

He looked like he was in his forties. He was wearing a suit and was heading quickly toward the bridge. I had an idea.

"If we get there at the same time as him, they won't be able to hassle us," I said.

"Maybe you're right," Oswald said.

We picked up our pace and timed it perfectly so that we got to one end of the wooden bridge as the man got onto the other. The punks were looking our way and hadn't even noticed him.

Two of the punks jumped off the railing so that they blocked the narrow path. They were both older and bigger than us.

"Where do you think you two are going?" the biggest one demanded.

"We're just going to school," Oswald mumbled.

"Looks like you're going to be late," the second added. The three others nodded their heads and chuckled.

"What's going on here?" the man asked. He was standing right behind the two punks, and they spun around.

"Nothing that concerns you, buddy," one of the punks snarled.

"First off," the man said, "I certainly am not your *buddy*, and second, it *is* my business. As is everything that happens at *my* school."

His school. What did that mean?

"My name is Mr. Roberts, and I'm the new principal."

New principal? We had a new principal?

"None of us go to this school," another of the punks said.

"How about you two?" he said, pointing at me and Oswald.

We both nodded.

"Then you two need to get to school and the rest of you need to leave."

"You can't tell us what to do, like he said, we don't go to your school."

"Then you have no business being on school property."

"This is public property," one of them said.

"No, *that's* public property," he said pointing to the end of the bridge where we had just come from. "This belongs to the school, so I think you better get off it, now!"

The other three jumped off the railing and onto their feet, but none of them seemed like they were getting ready to move. They just stood there, arms folded, facing him and away from us.

"Now, all of you smile," Mr. Roberts said.

Before anybody could react, he pulled out a camera, a flash went off, and he'd taken a picture.

"What are you doing?" one of them demanded.

"Gathering evidence," he said. "You have now been given notice that you are not allowed on school property. If I see you here again, you will be charged."

"You can't do that!" one of them screamed. "We're going to—"

Out of nowhere the man produced a large black baseball bat! He'd been holding it by his side, and I hadn't noticed. He slammed it against the wooden railing of the bridge, and all of us jumped into the air.

"Now, it's time you five got going," he said. "And please make sure to give your name to the two officers on your way."

He pointed across the bridge. Two uniformed cops were standing there, arms folded across their chests. They didn't look too friendly.

The five punks deflated and quietly walked past us in single file, eyes on the ground.

Oswald and I looked at each other, then at them and finally at Mr. Roberts, our new principal.

"And you two better get a move on or you'll have to get late slips."

"Yeah, sure," I said, unfreezing from my spot.

We started walking, and he walked with us.

"What are your names?" he asked.

"I'm Oswald."

"Oswald *Johnston*?" he said.

Oswald looked as surprised as I felt. How would he know who he was?

"There's only one Oswald in the school, so your name jumped out."

He reached out his hand, and Oswald hesitated for a split second before he realized that Mr. Roberts wanted to shake hands.

"I'm pleased to meet you, son," he said.

"Me too," Oswald mumbled.

He turned to me. "And you are?"

"Ian."

"Ian Cheevers?" he asked.

I startled slightly. "Yeah." How could he possibly know my name?

"You look surprised."

"It's just that there are a lot of people in the school named Ian."

"There are. I was just making a guess because the only Ian I know at the school is named Cheevers."

"You know me?"

"I always make it a point to know *every* student in my school within a month," he said. "And before the first day is over, I try to meet with every student who's ever been suspended."

Great. I get one suspension, last year, for three days, and it wasn't even my fault, and it wasn't that bad and—

"But I was also hoping to speak to you for another reason," he said.

"You were?"

"Yes, I also like to talk to all the school leaders."

"I'm not part of student government," I said.

He laughed. "I'll meet with them too, but I'm talking about the students who are the leaders among their peers."

"I'm no leader."

"After what you did to Frankie's, I'm not sure anybody would agree."

"Oh, you know about that."

"I think everybody in the whole school district knows about it," he said. "You two better get moving. The bell is about to go, and you are going to be late," he said.

"But...but we're here with you," Oswald said.

"I'm already at school. You two better get moving, fast!"

Oswald and I exchanged a look and started running.

"And, Ian!" he yelled.

I skidded to a stop and turned around. "Come and see me later today and we'll talk!"

I nodded and started running again. The bell was going to go any minute and I didn't want the next time I saw him to be for a late slip.

chapter five

I scanned the crowd, looking for Oswald and Julia. The whole school had been called to the auditorium for an assembly—an unplanned assembly. I'd heard lots of people mumbling and talking about what it was for, but I figured I already knew. We were going to be formally introduced to our new principal, Mr. Roberts.

"Ian!"

I turned. Julia and Oswald were waving their arms to get my attention. They were in the very first row. That was so Julia and so *not* Oswald. As the new school president she felt it was her obligation to be front and center. Oswald would have liked to have been off to the side.

It was also no surprise who won the argument about seating. They weren't dating anymore, but Julia was still firmly in charge. Julia was like a force of nature—strong, powerful, somewhat unpredictable and, if you weren't careful, you could get hurt.

"*I* know what this is about," Julia said, sounding smug.

"My guess is that it's about our new principal," Oswald said. The superior expression on Julia's face was replaced with a surprised look.

"You know about the new principal?" she questioned.

"Know about him? We've actually *met* him. But how do *you* know about the new principal?"

"I *am* the student president, remember? Ms. Hendricks told me."

Ms. Hendricks was our old principal. She really liked Julia.

"He seems like a pretty good guy," Oswald said.

"Yeah, he does," I agreed.

"Good guy," Julia said with a snort. "Shows how much you two know. I heard about what he was like at his old school."

"What was he like?" I asked.

"He ran the place like it was a military base."

I guessed that the baseball bat probably fit with that image.

Just then Ms. Hendricks, one of our vice-principals, Mr. Samuels, and Mr. Roberts walked onto the stage. I noticed that he didn't have his baseball bat with him.

Our principal—our *old* principal—took up a spot behind the podium.

"Good morning," Ms. Hendricks said into the microphone.

The crowd noise lessened but didn't stop completely.

"I'm sure you're wondering why you're here today."

"Some of you are aware that I am approaching retirement and that this is my last year," she said. "I was hoping to finish the year, but due to some personal issues it has become necessary to start my retirement now."

"Do you know what that's about?" I whispered to Julia.

"She told me her husband's been ill. He'll be okay, but he'll need some care for the next few months."

"So, today," Ms. Hendricks said, "I am saying good-bye and introducing you to your new principal, Mr. Roberts."

Ms. Hendricks clapped her hands, and there was a smattering of applause from the audience as he walked to the podium. He and Ms. Hendricks shook hands, and she walked over and took a seat.

"Thank you," he said. "Could we please have a round of applause for Ms. Hendricks."

This time it was louder, and there was some cheering. She was a good principal, and most people liked her.

"I am so pleased to be the new principal here," Mr. Roberts said. "I'm looking forward to getting to know all the staff and students, and I'm sure we'll all work together to make this school the best—"

He stopped midsentence. Had he forgotten what he was going to say? Was he having a seizure or—

"My parents always told me it was rude for me to talk while other people are talking, so I guess I should wait until those two boys at the back are finished with their discussion," he said.

I turned around, craned my neck and rose slightly in my seat to see who he was talking about. The last few rows were filled with potential candidates. It could have been any of twenty guys occupying those seats.

Every school has a core group of people—usually guys—who cause all the trouble. I was actually surprised that ours were even here at the assembly. Usually they used assemblies as an excuse to go out and have a smoke.

"I'll continue," he said. "I know that there have been some issues with your school."

He made it sound like we were a problem school. Sure, the last couple of years there had been talk about how we didn't have enough discipline at this school and how badly we behaved at football games and dances and things like that. And then there'd been a couple of incidents of vandalism and a bunch of laptop computers were stolen and...Well, maybe we did have issues.

"But I believe that this school has the potential to be the *very* best in the district if we're all prepared to work together to make it happen. What I need from each and every one of you is to make a commitment to—"

He stopped talking again, walked to the front of the stage, jumped off and started up the aisle. Every eye followed him. He stopped at the last row.

"I am so *sorry* that I keep disturbing you two boys and interrupting your conversation," he said. "But you just keep on talking. I'll wait. I'm an incredibly patient man. No, that's a lie. I have never been patient with rude. You two, stand up, *now*!" he yelled.

Two boys stumbled to their feet. I knew them. Everybody knew them. They were making high school a seven-year project—assuming they ever did graduate.

"These two boys," Mr. Roberts said as he turned and faced the auditorium, "do *not* run the school. They have no *right* to disrespect *me* or anybody *else* in this school. They will show respect for *everybody* in this school, or they will not be *in* this school."

He turned to face the two boys and moved so close that he was practically on top of them. He was such a big man that he towered over them. He didn't need that baseball bat to be scary.

"You boys have a problem with what I'm saying?"

They both shook their heads and mumbled answers that I couldn't hear.

"Sit down," Mr. Roberts ordered, and they dropped down like they'd been shot.

I was really starting to like this guy. As

he walked back toward the stage, there was a rumble of reaction.

"Man, this guy doesn't take prisoners," I whispered to Oswald.

"If he does, it's just to execute them. Remind me not to get him mad at me."

As he walked past us, he looked in our direction. "Ian, Oswald, good to see you," he said quietly.

Before we could respond, he bounded up onto the stage.

"I told you we knew him," Oswald said to Julia.

"Now, as I was saying before I was interrupted, I expect every person in this school to be respected by every other person. Respect is one of the few things that is *given*, but that has to be *earned*. It's one of the few things that if you want to *receive* it, you have to *give* it."

He paused and looked around the room. There wasn't a sound.

"Everybody in this school is going to be working toward the same goal. And anybody who isn't—students," he said, gesturing to the audience, "or staff"—he said as he looked at the teachers assembled on the stage—"will quickly find they will not be part of this school."

I looked at the expressions of some of the teachers. Some seemed to be surprised by his comment, others angry, and more than a few looked afraid. A couple nodded in agreement, including Mr. Phillips. He was the guy who had me suspended last year. He was also the teacher I respected the most in the whole school.

"People who aren't willing to work together are not welcome. No exceptions, no excuses, no reason to accept failure." He paused. "Are there any questions?"

Julia's hand shot up instantly. He motioned to her.

"I was wondering what role—"

"Excuse me," Mr. Roberts said, cutting her off. "Could you please stand up and state your name."

"Yeah, sure," she said and got to her feet. "My name is Julia Brown—and I'm the student president."

"Pleased to meet you, Ms. Brown," he said. He walked to the edge of the stage, bent down and offered his hand. They shook.

"While we are all equally important, it is nice to meet somebody who has taken the initiative to take on a leadership role. I respect people who are leaders. Please, your question."

"In your last school you made a lot of changes," Julia said. "Will you be consulting with student government before making changes here?"

"I'll talk to anybody who wants to talk."

"So your door is open to the student president?"

"My door is always open to you, as it is to all students. The president part is not as important to me as the student part."

"But as the president I represent the students at the—"

"I'm hoping students will feel free to represent themselves."

"But I was democratically elected."

"It's important to remember one thing. This is not a democracy. We're not having a vote or counting the ballots."

"But if all the students want one thing and you want another, don't you think that it makes sense that you should change your position?"

"Just because something is popular doesn't make it right, and because something is right won't always make it popular. In the end, I'm going to do what I think is right, whether you agree or not."

Julia looked angry and confused, as if she wanted to say something, but she just didn't know what to say. Julia at a loss for words—what a concept.

"Are there questions from *anybody* else?" Mr. Roberts asked.

Julia continued to stand there for a few seconds. She suddenly looked embarrassed—she knew she'd been dismissed in front of the whole school. She slumped down into her seat.

I was really, *really* starting to like this guy.

chapter six

Julia slammed her tray onto the table, and some of her soup sloshed out of the bowl. She took the seat beside Oswald.

"I really don't like that man," Julia said.

Oswald shot me a look. We knew who she was talking about. We'd just been talking about how we liked him, but you'd have to be stupid to mention that to her right now.

"I like him," Oswald said.

Okay, maybe not stupid but determined to try to tick her off. Oswald actually seemed to like doing that. For that brief time they'd been together, he'd agreed with everything she said. He'd spent the last five months making up for that.

"No," Oswald said, "not just like. I really, *really* like him."

"I can't believe that anybody would like him...except for you."

"Maybe not just me. What do you think, Ian?"

Setup. "It's a little early for me to make a judgment, one way or the other. I'd need more information."

I smirked at Oswald. He shot, I dodged.

"Well, let me tell you more about him," Julia said. "He's a former sergeant in the marines."

"Former?" I asked. "I think once you're a marine, you're always a marine."

"Well, he does like to run schools like they're a military base," she said. "For example, at his last school he banned the use of cell phones."

"Lots of schools have done that," I

argued. "Kids were using them to text message answers to each other during tests."

"That's just an excuse. Just don't allow them on during tests. He also banned iPods."

My hand instinctively went down to touch the pocket where my iPod was.

"And once he banned them, he started to take them away from kids whenever he saw one," she said. "That can't even be legal."

"I don't think he'd do anything illegal," Oswald said.

"He did give them back at the end of the year," she admitted. "Along with all the hats he took. If a kid wore a hat, he took it."

"If he takes hats, then don't wear a hat," I said.

"He also did random locker searches," she said.

"Who cares? He can look in my locker any time he wants," Oswald said. "He doesn't need my permission."

"What he'd need to search your locker is a gas mask," I said. "Are you ever going to wash your gym clothes?"

"They're aging. Like a fine wine or cheese."

"I guess it's working. They smell sort of like cheese."

"Would you two stop!" Julia snapped. "I'm trying to be serious."

"You don't have to *try* to be serious," I said under my breath.

"What?"

"Nothing," I said. Nothing I wanted to repeat.

"And that 'my-door-is-always-open' line of his is just that, a line," she said. "I tried to go and see him earlier, and his door was not only closed, but the secretary said he was going to be busy all day."

Oswald started to laugh.

"What's so funny?" Julia asked.

I knew what was so funny. It was better coming from me than him.

"I was in his office before lunch," I said.

"You? What were you doing in his office?" Julia demanded. "Were you in trouble?"

"No, of course not. He just wanted to talk to me."

"What did he want to talk to you about?"

"Lots of things," I said, trying to be vague. "You know, about the whole thing with Frankie's and me being suspended before that."

"And don't forget the leadership part," Oswald said.

I felt like reaching out and smacking him, but he was too far across the table.

"What does that mean?" Julia said.

I really didn't want to answer, but there wasn't much choice.

"He thinks that there are leaders in the school."

"Like student council," Julia said.

I shrugged. "Right, yeah. But he also thinks that there are other people who can be leaders. He thinks I'm one of them."

Julia started to laugh, and I instantly felt offended.

"You don't think I can be a leader?"

"I think you *could* be a leader," she said.

"Could?"

"That Frankie's thing proved you can be a great leader. But maybe that was only a fluke. You refused to even run for student council."

"I didn't want to run for council."

"You don't want to do anything lately except hang around, watch TV, play video games and do those stupid flash mob things."

"Mr. Roberts doesn't think flash mobs are stupid," I said.

They both looked at me with surprise. "We were just talking and I mentioned them to him. I don't know why. It just slipped out, and then he wanted to know more. He said they sounded interesting."

"Not interesting. Stupid," Julia said.

"Flash mobs are not nearly as stupid as student government!" Oswald protested.

"Student government is not stupid—"

"Flash mobs don't *have* to be stupid," I said, cutting Julia off.

Oswald and Julia looked at me.

"It's just that I have an idea for a new flash mob."

"Count me in," Oswald said.

"And count me out," Julia added.

"I wasn't thinking you'd be part of it," I said. "But I was hoping you could film it, as sort of a favor."

She shrugged. "Sure, I guess I could do that."

chapter seven

"I can't believe that you're not going to tell me what this is all about," Julia said.

"Don't you like surprises?" I asked.

"You *know* I hate surprises."

"Really?" I did know that, but bothering her was so appealing.

"Don't tell her," Oswald said.

He was much more obvious about trying to annoy her.

"It's not like she's actually participating in the flash mob," he said.

"But I am taping it," she said.

"That's why he shouldn't tell you," Oswald continued. "You're just taping, it's not like you need to know what we're going to do. You just have to point the camera at us and push the button."

"He's right," I agreed. "But make sure you start wide-frame so you can get the big red neon sign in. Then go down to the action on the street, and after we all take off, go wide again."

"Are you hoping to be a film director some day?" Julia asked.

"I just want it done right, okay?"

She saluted.

"Thank you." I looked at my watch. We had six minutes. "We better get going," I said to Oswald.

"Showtime."

We left Julia up on the balcony of the neighboring building. It overlooked where we were going to be—a nice vantage point to tape the event.

We hit the street. Traffic was rushing by—cars on the road and people on the sidewalk.

It was very busy and very public. That gave it more potential—for good or bad. More people could take part, more people could watch and more people might get mad.

"I hope this works. Nothing would be worse than nobody coming."

"Nobody coming wouldn't be the worst," Oswald said.

"What would?"

"Having only a few people come. If nobody shows, we can just walk away."

I shook my head. "I'm not walking away if there's only me and you."

"There'll be more than just us. I've seen a couple of familiar faces," he said.

"That's good...I guess."

"And if it does crash and burn, you have Julia up there filming it. You know she'll never let you forget about it."

"I know."

"Why did you invite her anyway?" Oswald asked.

I shook my head. "I'm not sure. I guess I'm just trying to include her because she's our friend."

"That's right. *Friend*. Keep it that way."

I cringed slightly but didn't answer. Did he know more than I thought he knew?

I looked down at my watch. Two minutes. We walked right to the spot underneath the big red sign—the neon sign that showed that this building was owned by a gigantic tobacco company. There were a half dozen men and women outside the main doors, smoking. At least they believed in what they were selling. I didn't know whether that meant they had integrity or were just really stupid.

On the sidewalk, men in suits and ties carrying briefcases, and women in business outfits with purses over their shoulders, raced by in both directions, shoulder to shoulder. Oswald and I formed two rocks in the stream, and we were repeatedly bumped as people tried to get by us.

Around us were dozens of kids—our age or a few years older—who weren't going anywhere. They were all trying to act casual and not look at each other. They wouldn't have to wait long.

The alarm on my watch started to beep. It was time.

I brought my fingers up to my lips and put the invisible cigarette into my mouth. I took in a big puff of imaginary smoke. I looked around. There were thirty—no, forty or fifty—people all doing the same. We formed a big dam in the middle of the river of commuters, trying to get by as we continued to "smoke."

Then Oswald's watch started to beep. We dropped our invisible cigarettes to the ground and stomped them out. After Oswald and I started to cough, people all around us started to cough and hack. It was an incredible noise.

I caught the look in the eyes of those trying to rush by us. Some looked worried, as if we had some virus they might catch.

My watch went off a second time, and I fell to the concrete. In the split second of my fall, I saw other people collapse all around me.

I couldn't move—I was "dead"—a victim of smoking. But I tried to look at the scene with one partially opened eye. I couldn't see the people on the ground, but I could see the circle of people standing, mouths open, staring down at us. It was a big circle, so there must have been a lot of dead people lying on the sidewalk.

I closed my eye and tried to picture the circle growing, as more and more people who were trying to get home were blocked and backed up. It would have been so cool to see the whole thing as it was happening. Julia would have a great angle, so we'd be able to see it when we watched the tape.

I'd expected there to be a lot of noise, but it seemed remarkably quiet. The only sounds were those of the passing cars. I had to fight the urge to sit up and look around. The ground was starting to feel cold, and I was starting to get nervous. It had to be longer than a minute by now, for sure. Had Oswald's watch gone wrong, or had it gone off and I hadn't heard it and everybody else had left already? I opened one eye. There were still bodies all around me, including Oswald.

The alarm sounded—the second one from Oswald's watch—and I jumped to my feet. Everybody else got to theirs at the same instant. We broke through the circle and started to melt into the crowd. It was easy because now that the dam had been broken, the whole crowd started to surge forward.

I realized that half of the mob was moving in our direction. There wasn't much choice. The six lanes of traffic hemmed us in on one side and the building hemmed us in on the other, so there were only the two ways to go.

We'd gone only a half dozen steps when I was startled by the sight of two uniformed police officers coming toward us. They were moving quickly, and they looked very serious.

"Just keep walking," I hissed. "Don't look at them, eyes straight forward."

We shifted off to the side, as did the rest of the crowd, allowing the two officers to steam on past us.

"Nothing to it," I said as we continued to walk.

We hit the stairs and headed toward Julia and the video. I couldn't wait to see both of them.

chapter eight

I opened my book to the right page. I had to at least look like I was following along as the teacher kept babbling on.

I knew this stuff pretty well. Actually I had almost a ninety in history so I knew this stuff *really* well. It was just that I had other things on my mind right now. The only history that really interested me was more recent—yesterday.

Oswald and I had been up till almost two in the morning going over the digital tape.

We'd watched it a half dozen times. It was more than good. It was nothing short of great.

I'd paused the tape so we could count the bodies on the ground. It was hard to tell in some places where one body stopped and the next started, but we'd done a rough count and got at least thirty people on the ground and four times as many in the circle that had surrounded us.

It was just like I'd imagined, the crowd getting bigger and bigger as we blocked traffic. There were hundreds of them.

I couldn't help but wonder if any of the people in the crowd had figured out what we were doing: showing how smoking cigarettes led to death. It was a flash mob, but it was a flash mob with meaning.

Julia had done a great job on the camera. Shockingly she'd done what I'd asked, so the big, red, neon, tobacco company sign was the start and the end of the event. Just before she shifted back to the sign, she'd kept focused on the spot where the "die-in" had taken place. It showed those two police officers we'd passed and two others coming from the other direction. They'd met in the middle, almost exactly where we'd been lying down. Thirty seconds longer and we would have looked up to see them standing over us. Timing was everything. I'd made a mental note to make sure that future flash mobs that I organized never went on for very long.

The whole thing had been such a success, even Julia had been impressed. Well, maybe impressed wasn't quite the right word. She'd said that it wasn't *completely* stupid. For her that was practically a compliment.

The bell rang, signaling the end of the morning and the start of lunch. I wanted lunch.

The hall was crowded. Everybody rushed to get to lunch. Well, not everybody. Lots of people were just standing around talking, getting in my way.

I passed by the office and looked through the glass windows. Just then Mr. Roberts' door flew open and Julia came out. She looked angry. No, not angry—enraged.

I wanted to duck or hide or get out of her way, but she'd already seen me.

She stomped over, bumping into a girl on her way.

"That *man* makes me *so* angry," she snorted.

"Mr. Roberts?"

"Who else do you think I'd be talking about?"

I shrugged. "Lots of people make you angry."

"Didn't I warn you about him?" she asked.

"Well, you—"

"Didn't I tell you he'd take away phones and iPods and hats?"

"You did say—"

"Do you know what he's doing now?"

I didn't answer. No point in being interrupted, or was I interrupting her rant?

"Don't you want to know?" she demanded.

"Oh, am I allowed to talk now? So what did he do now?"

"He's canceling the school dances."

"We have school dances?"

"Of course we have school—"

She stopped midsentence, realizing that I was chirping her. I knew we had dances. I had just never gone to one and neither had she.

"He didn't consult with anybody. Not staff, not students and not student council."

I was going to say, not the student *president*, but that would have been pretty obvious.

"He must have had a reason," I said.

"For not consulting anyone, or for canceling the dances?" she asked.

"Maybe both, but probably the dance part. Did he say why he was doing it?"

"He said something about students not being responsible...bad behavior, alcohol and fights."

"Weren't a bunch of students suspended for drinking, fighting and vandalizing cars after the last dance?"

"Well, yes, but those are not excuses to cancel the dance."

"Sounds like some pretty good excuses."

"Whose side are you on anyway?" she demanded.

"I didn't think I was on a side."

"Well, you *should* be. This is important."

"Yeah right," I said sarcastically. "High school dances rank right up there with world hunger, war, poverty, child abuse and—"

"You don't understand," she said as if she was talking to a five-year-old.

"When did dances become so important to you?" I asked.

"It's not the dance. It's the *principle* of the thing."

"The principle or the principal?"

"What?" she snapped. "What are you talking about?"

"The principle, like what you believe in, or the principal, like Mr. Roberts?"

She didn't answer.

"He's just trying to get some control."

"I don't call it control. I call it controlling. Do you even know how many people he's suspended in the three weeks since he took over?"

"How many?"

"Over forty."

"Some of the people who were suspended should have been suspended. Did you like kids hassling other students in the halls? Do you think there should be fights in the cafeteria? Did you like the gang down by the bridge? Do you really think there *should* be drinking and fighting at school dances?"

"I guess that answers the question about whose side you're on."

"I'm just saying that some of the things he's done have made the school better... safer...calmer."

"You don't understand."

There was that tone again.

"Some things are worth fighting for," she said.

"And school dances are one of those things?"

"Not being told what we can and cannot do is one of them," she argued.

"It's a school. Most of what happens here is about being told what to do. This isn't a democracy."

She let out a little scream, and I startled as people walking by all turned and stared.

"Now you're quoting him. That's just sick. Is he your hero?"

"Now you're just being stupid."

Although he *had* been like a hero out there on the bridge that first day. All he needed was a cape to go along with the baseball bat. What was wrong with him taking care of business?

"I'm not going to stand for it," Julia said.

"And what exactly does that mean?"

"I'm going to...going to...I don't really know."

I almost laughed but thought better of it.

"Do you have any ideas?" she asked.

Now I did laugh. "Me? What makes you think I want to get involved in any of this?"

"Because you're my friend. Besides, wasn't I right there when you organized the boycott of Frankie's Fast—"

She stopped mid-sentence, and a smile started to form on her face, getting bigger and more smug-looking.

"That's it," she said. "I'm going to do what you did with Frankie's."

"You're going to organize a boycott of a dance that isn't happening?"

"Don't be stupid. I'm going to organize a boycott of school."

chapter nine

I double-clicked on the MSN icon, and
the screen opened up. I started to enter
my password, typing in the first three
letters of my dog Shadow's name, before I
remembered that that wasn't my password
anymore.

I'd read that pet names were the first
thing people tried when they wanted to
get into your e-mail, so I figured I should
change it. Yeah, like my Hotmail account
was important enough for somebody to

try to hack into. Whole groups of spies, terrorists and international criminals were trying to find out who I was talking to.

Regardless I had changed it to something nobody would ever guess. I typed it in: *J-u-l-i-a*. I figured nobody would ever figure that one out. I certainly hoped that Julia or Oswald would never know.

I hit Enter and scrolled down to my contact list. Julia wasn't online, but Oswald was.

hey Oz, I typed.

what u doing? he replied.

homework. u?

nm

That was code for nothing much.

has j been on line? I asked.

nope...you seen her Facebook event?

she created an event? I asked.

she's doing a school boycott event, he replied.

I'd hoped that she'd just forget about that whole idea. Although, knowing Julia the way I did, I didn't think that was too likely.

she also wrote about Roberts in the event description, Oz wrote.

what did she publish? I asked.

she let him have it...she hates him!

I felt a tingle go up my spine. What exactly had she written? I had to look.

gtg...see u l8r, I typed, and then I clicked off the page.

I minimized my MSN and logged onto Facebook. There was an invite to Julia's boycott. I clicked on her profile. There was a picture of her smirking, with her two cats on her lap. It was a really nice picture, and I couldn't help but smile to myself as I looked at her.

I started to scroll down to look for something about...I didn't have to go far.

There it was under "Notes."

You don't have to go to some foreign country to find out about dictators. Just visit our school. This man—this principal without principles—is dangerous, mostly because he is a chest-thumping ape too stupid to even realize how stupid he is. I've had enough of his tirades, of him playing macho-man, telling us what to do. It was bad enough when he took away cell phones and iPods and hats, but now he's taking away our right to free assembly, our dance. You've probably all heard that he canceled the school dance. Maybe he did it because he can't dance or because nobody would dance with him when he was in high school. Who can blame them?

We don't have to take it any more. We don't have to take his evil ways. I'm not going to be told what to do by some mouth-breathing jerk. I'm going to stand up to fight him, and you can too. How?

Next Friday, the day when the dance is supposed to be held, I'm not going to school. If I can't go to the school dance, then I'm not going to school! NONE of us should go to school!

Go to a friend's house, the mall, play football in the park, play video games, watch TV, sleep in. And you'll not just be having fun but striking a blow against tyrants. We'll be teaching this evil man more of a lesson than he'll ever teach us.

And don't worry about getting in trouble. If we all do it—everybody in the whole school— then nobody can get in trouble...well, just one person can...that twerp of a principal. With any luck we can drive him out of the school and back under the rock he climbed out from.

Tell your friends, tell everybody. Together we can defeat him!

Oh, this was not good.

I grabbed the phone and dialed Julia's number. She picked up on the first ring.

"Hey, Ian," she said, before I could even say hello. I hated Caller ID.

"Julia, are you insane?" I snapped.

"I prefer the term eccentric, but what are you talking about specifically?"

"Facebook. Are you crazy? You can't write stuff like that about the principal."

"Sure I can. There's a little thing called freedom of speech. Ever hear of it?" she said sarcastically.

"Yeah, I know about freedom of speech. Do you know anything about slander, libel and lawsuits? Have you ever heard of any of those?"

"Lawsuits don't scare me," she said.

"They should."

"Did it scare you when Frankie's threatened to sue you?"

"Of course it scared me," I admitted. "And as I recall it scared you too."

"But they didn't actually do it," she said.

"No, but that was only because I didn't write anything that wasn't true."

"Neither did *I*," she said.

"You called him a stupid mouth-breathing dictator."

"Like I said, I didn't write anything that wasn't true."

"Julia, you have to take that note off your page. You have to cancel the event or you'll get in trouble, big trouble."

"I'm not taking it down. Matter of fact, I've sent out invitations to everybody I could think of to join my page. I've already added over seventy new friends since I posted it. Soon everybody in the whole school will know about it."

"Great, just great. So more and more people will see it."

"Isn't that the idea?" she questioned. "The more people who see it, the more people who can get involved. Sort of like those stupid flash mobs of yours, except mine has a purpose."

"And is that purpose to get you suspended?"

"If everybody joins the boycott, he can't suspend us all."

"No, but he could suspend the person who *started* it."

"How is he going to find out I started it?"

"Julia, that *w-w-w* does stand for World Wide Web, as in anybody in the whole world can see it. You know that, right?" I asked sarcastically.

"I also know that the only people who can see my Facebook page are friends I allow in, and there's no way he's a friend of mine. Not like some people I know."

I understood that shot was aimed at me, but I wasn't going to get caught by it.

"You really don't understand," I said. "It's not as simple as that. There are people who are friends of your friends who—"

"Are you planning to show it to him?" she asked.

"Me?"

"Yeah, he's such a good friend of yours that I figured you'd call him up at home and tell him."

"I'm not going to tell him anything, but believe me, he'll find out soon enough."

"I don't care if he finds out," she said. "I actually hope he does." She paused. "So, are you going to walk out? Are you going to join the boycott?"

"I've never even been to a school dance," I said. "I don't think it's really that big a—"

"I guess you've answered my question," she snapped.

"I haven't answered anything yet—"

There was a dial tone. She'd hung up on me! She'd cut me off before I could tell her that even though I didn't believe in it, I'd still walk out because she *was* my friend and not some stupid Facebook friend.

I put down the phone and picked it up to call her back and tell her. I held onto the phone for a few seconds, and then I put the receiver down. I picked it up again and put it down once more. Forget it.

chapter ten

There was a buzz around the school when I arrived in the morning. Less than twelve hours had passed and everybody seemed to know. That was the power and the danger of the Internet.

I heard that Julia had added over two hundred new friends to her Facebook. At least that's what Oswald told me. I didn't speak to Julia all morning. I saw her down at the end of the hall and waved, but she was surrounded by people and didn't wave back. I wasn't sure if she was blowing me off or if she simply didn't see me because she was so busy being the center of things. She'd like that.

I waded through the cafeteria and joined Oswald at our table in the corner. Julia was probably still doing her star turn.

"Hey, Oz," I said, sitting down beside him.

"Nice to have a little company. Probably just the two of us."

"Who knows, Julia may join us," I said.

"She might join me, but I doubt she'll even sit down if you're here."

My eyes opened in shock, and I turned to face him. "Come on, she's not that angry."

"Have you seen her Facebook event?"

"Of course. That's why she's so mad because I told her she shouldn't be saying those things about Roberts."

"I don't mean the comments about him. I meant the comments about *you*."

"Me? She's written a note about me?"

"She doesn't really say it's you. She doesn't mention you by name," he said.

I was confused. "I don't get it. If she doesn't mention me, how do you know she's writing about me?"

"Just a guess."

"What did she write?" I demanded angrily.

He held up his hands. "Remember, it wasn't me who wrote it."

"What did she write?" I repeated.

"That some people are just too sucky, too much like little babies to join the boycott."

"What makes you think she's writing about me?"

"Well, she also wrote that one of her friends was like Roberts' little puppy dog and that he was afraid of cutting school that day."

"She wrote that?" I demanded.

"That's sort of the *Reader's Digest* version. I doubt people even know it's you she's talking about."

"Maybe it's not me."

"Julia only has two close friends, and I'm going to join the boycott."

"Do you really care about the school dance?" I asked.

He laughed. "I'm willing to walk out of school for almost *any* reason." He paused. "I'm just not sure why you don't want to walk out."

"I didn't say I wasn't going to."

"So you *are* going to join the boycott?" he asked.

"I didn't say that either."

"The problem is that if you join it now, it'll look like Julia has you whipped."

I knew what he was saying. I'd been thinking the same thing.

"I just don't know why this is such a big deal for her. He's taken away other things more important than a dance," I said.

Oswald shook his head. "She's upset because she was going to the dance with somebody."

"What?"

"She had a date."

"With you?" I gasped.

"Do you think I'm crazy...crazier... crazy *again*?"

"Sorry, I just thought that maybe—"

"That maybe I'd lost my mind again?" he asked.

I shrugged.

"Dating Julia *once* was more than enough. She's going with Trevor."

"Trevor who?"

"Trevor Maclean. He asked her to the dance."

I knew him. He was older, in grade twelve, and on the football team.

"So, if there's no dance, there's no Trevor," Oswald said. "That's why she's upset. Losing the dance would mean losing the chance to go out with him."

"I didn't even know she liked him," I said.

"She wouldn't tell you," he said. "She tells *me* things like that. And do you know why she tells me these things and not you?"

"Because you're the *bestest girl*friend she ever had," I answered sarcastically.

"She tells *me* because I'm her old boyfriend and she likes to rub it in. She doesn't tell *you* because she still hopes that someday you *will* be her boyfriend."

I tried to hide the surprise. "Yeah right, like that's going to happen."

"You have to admit that you've thought about it," he said.

For a fleeting second I considered telling him about our half-date, but thought better.

"I've thought about never talking to her again, but that isn't going to happen either," I said.

"I can tell you from experience, if you do date her, you *really* will think about that."

There was a loud buzzing sound as the PA came to life.

"Attention, please." It was Mr. Roberts. I'd never heard him on the PA before. I didn't have a good feeling about it.

The noise in the cafeteria faded, but not everybody was paying attention.

"Everybody stop!" he yelled. "All talking, all walking, all teaching, everything stop!"

The cafeteria became eerily quiet.

"It has come to my attention that there is a planned boycott of school."

It had taken less than a day for him to become aware of it. I wasn't surprised.

"I want to advise students against taking part in this protest. There are consequences for any action in life, and I want you all to be aware that the consequence for this will be a three-day suspension."

"He can't give the whole school a three-day suspension," Oswald said as the cafeteria buzzed with conversation.

"And," Mr. Roberts continued, "you have my word that *all* students taking part will receive that punishment. If there are one hundred students, then one hundred students will be suspended. If there are four hundred, it will be very quiet around here as four hundred students will be gone for three days. I hope it will not be necessary for me to suspend anybody else."

Oswald and I looked at each other, and I knew we were both thinking the same thing—*anybody else*. We now knew why Julia wasn't here.

chapter eleven

I sat at the computer, and both of my parents looked over my shoulder—at Julia's Facebook.

"She didn't pull any punches," my father said.

"That girl certainly has spirit," my mother added.

"And guts," my father agreed.

"What she *has* is a five-day suspension," I said.

"She was lucky to get off that lightly," my father said.

"You think five days is light?" I questioned.

"First off, she publicly insulted and attacked your principal."

"And she tried to get everybody to cut school," my mother added. "That's not just breaking the rules but asking others to break rules. I must admit that I'm a little disappointed."

"I guess her parents must be really disappointed," I said.

"I meant in *you*," my mother said.

"Me?" I exclaimed.

"Yes, you should have talked her out of this."

"I tried to talk her out of it! She wouldn't listen!"

"Then you should have tried harder, been more convincing," my mother continued.

"You don't understand," I protested. "Here, let me show you."

I scrolled down to the spot where she insulted me.

"Oh, my dear," my mother said. "She was

really, really angry with you," she commented as she read down the page.

"Is she still angry?" my father asked.

"I don't know. She's not allowed to take phone calls or go on the computer."

"So you don't even know how she's doing," my father said.

"I know how she's doing," I said. "She's probably feeling just awful."

Julia and I had been in school together since grade school, and I couldn't remember her even having a detention before.

"I imagine that the boycott is off," my mother said.

"Completely dead."

"I'm not surprised. Your principal cut the head off the snake," my father said. "Not that I'm calling Julia a snake. It's just a saying. You take away the leadership, the head."

"No, I understand. Without a leader, things just fizzle."

"Unless somebody else becomes the leader, steps in and—" My mother stopped mid-sentence. "You're not planning on becoming that leader, are you?"

"He'd just suspend you too," my father added before I could answer.

"I wasn't even sure I was going to take part in the boycott," I said to reassure them.

My mother let out a sigh. "That's good to know...very reassuring."

"I just don't think school dances are that big a deal."

"They're not," my father agreed. "Of course this has less to do with school dances and more to do with your friend trying to stand up and then being suspended."

"It almost sounds like you're trying to talk him *into* doing something," my mother snapped.

"Of course I'm not," he protested.

He spun me around in my seat and looked me squarely in the eyes. "Give me your word you won't do anything that will get you in trouble, get you suspended."

"Sure, you have my word."

My mother reached down and gave me a little hug.

"Good," my father said. "Let's have supper."

"I'll be up in a minute," I said.

My parents left my room, leaving me alone with Julia's Facebook page. She was there on the screen, smiling at me. She probably wasn't smiling now. Why hadn't she listened to me? She was suspended, and there was nothing I could do about it. Well, there was nothing I could do about the suspension, but still, there might be something I *could* do.

chapter twelve

The lunch bell rang, and I jumped out of my seat and sprinted out of the room. I was almost in the hall before the ringing stopped echoing off the wall. I slung my backpack over my shoulder and ran along the hall and down the steps, taking them three at a time. I pushed open the door and ran to where Oswald was going to meet me. I didn't have to wait long. He came charging around the side of the building at a full run.

He skidded to a stop in front of me.

"Are you sure you want to do this?" he asked.

"Pretty sure. The worst thing that can happen is I get suspended."

"Wrong," Oswald said. "The worst thing that can happen is that *I* get suspended."

I couldn't help but laugh.

"A suspension for me would be a death sentence," he continued.

"Don't be such a drama queen."

"I'm not. My parents would kill me."

"I'll make sure that if anybody gets suspended it's me. I'm totally responsible. We better get moving."

We started across the parking lot, toward the bridge.

"I don't know if I'd be so helpful if she'd written those things about me," Oswald said.

"This isn't about Julia."

He snorted. "Sure it's not."

"It isn't. Besides, even if I wanted to stop it now I don't think I could. Look around."

There was a stream of kids, some in

front, but most behind us, heading for the bridge. It looked like there were already thirty or forty people in the field on the other side of the bridge.

"Mr. Roberts isn't going to like this," Oswald said.

"That's the point."

I stopped at the bridge, stepping aside, and dropped my backpack to the ground. I opened it up and pulled out the bullhorn I'd borrowed from the gym department. The gym teacher hadn't asked what I needed it for.

I put it up to my mouth and pushed the button. It buzzed slightly.

"Please move across the bridge," I said. "Make sure you keep all banned items in your bag or in your pockets until you get over the bridge."

The lines of people streaming out of the school all came together, funneling into one line to cross the bridge. There were a lot of kids. Hundreds and hundreds. That was good. Well, good if I wanted to get Mr. Roberts' attention. I guess that was the point of this flash mob.

Kids kept passing by. I knew a lot of them, but there were a lot I didn't know. It seemed like everybody knew *me* though. So many kids said hello, or yelled out or just gave me the thumbs-up. Everybody seemed really happy, as if they were heading to a party. That made sense. It was sort of a party.

Kids kept coming out of the school, but the crest of the wave had already passed by. It was time for me to get over there and start leading.

"Come on," I said to Oswald. "I wonder how many kids there—"

"I counted over nine hundred," Oswald replied.

"Come on, you're kidding, right?"

"Not kidding. Counting is one of my skills. I'm not just a pretty face, you know."

"So, nine hundred kids out of a population of less than fifteen hundred is almost two-thirds of the entire school."

"Almost, but there are *more* than nine hundred. That doesn't count the kids who were already over there before I started counting, and there are more coming. Probably more like seventy-five percent of the school is already out here. Pretty impressive for less than a day of planning."

"The beauty of flash mobs."

We crossed the bridge, and I climbed up onto a garbage can, using it like a stage. I put the bullhorn up to my mouth.

"Can I have your attention!" I called out.

Everybody stopped talking and laughing and moving and looked at me.

"Thank you all for coming out to our unofficial school dance."

A gigantic cheer went up, and people waved their hands in the air.

"Enjoy yourselves, dance to your music and be kind to each other, and we'll give you a signal when it's time to head back to school."

"What if we don't want to head back to school?" a boy yelled out, and others cheered.

"You can do what you want," I answered. "But I hope everybody will head back. It'll send a message about who we are, about how we can have a dance. Okay, everybody get ready."

All around me people pulled their iPods out of pockets and pouches and purses.

"Enjoy the dance!" I yelled.

Everybody all around put the buds in their ears, turned on their iPods and began dancing to their own music!

Standing on top of the garbage can, I was able to take in the whole scene. There were about a thousand kids, all plugged in to their own music, dancing to hundreds of different tunes, all without a single sound—a silent dance.

I jumped down from the garbage can and set down the bullhorn. Oswald climbed up onto the can, taking my place. He pulled out his video camera and started to film.

I removed my iPod from my pocket, clipped on the headphones and pushed Play. John Legend came through the earbuds, and I started to dance as well. I might as well enjoy the moment—no telling how it was going to end.

chapter thirteen

The dance was amazing, everybody doing their own thing. Some danced fast, some slow, some wild, all grooving to their own tunes—sounds that nobody else could hear. Sometimes people exchanged iPods. Sometimes there were couples—either a boy and a girl or a couple of girls—who each had one earbud from the same iPod and were listening to the same song, dancing to the same beat.

When I wasn't watching the crowd, I

kept an eye on the school, waiting for Mr. Roberts to appear. Part of me wanted him to come out. The other part wanted him to stay away, either unaware or ignoring what was going on out here. That would have been easier, but what would have been the point? Then, almost like I'd magically made him appear, he did. He walked across the parking lot toward the bridge. It was a slow, deliberate walk.

I gestured for Oswald, got his attention and pointed toward the school. He saw Mr. Roberts too and jumped down off the garbage can. I couldn't blame him for not wanting to stand head and shoulders above the crowd. It would be much better to just blend in. I wished I had that choice.

I kept my iPod playing and I kept dancing, but I danced toward the bridge. I wanted to be there when he crossed.

He came across the parking lot by himself. He moved with confidence, no hesitation. As he got closer, I was relieved to see that he wasn't carrying his baseball bat—not that I really thought he would be, but just the same, I'd wondered.

He stopped in the middle of the bridge, the spot where school property ended. He stood there, looking out at the scene of most of the students from his school, dancing. I would have paid to know what he was thinking. Then he looked at me, locking his eyes on mine. He started toward me. I wasn't going to have to pay to find out what was on his mind.

He stopped directly in front of me. I pulled out my earbuds.

"Good afternoon, Ian," he said. His voice was calm.

"Hello, sir," I said. Showing respect couldn't hurt.

"I assume this is all your doing."

"Why would you think that?" I asked.

"Who else could organize a flash mob like this except you?" he asked.

For a split second I thought about denying it, but I knew there was no point.

I nodded. "I did it."

"You given any thought to how this might end?" he asked.

"I know exactly how it'll end."

"You do?" He sounded surprised.

"Yeah." I looked at my watch. "In thirteen minutes Oswald is going to use the bullhorn to tell everybody that the dance is over, and everybody will go back to school."

"That's good to know," he said. "And do you know how it's going to end for *you*?"

"I'm going back to school with everybody else."

"Are you?"

His question sent a shiver up my spine. I had to stay calm.

"Why wouldn't I go back to school?"

"Have you thought about the possibility of a suspension?" he asked.

I swallowed hard. "I thought about it, and I don't think you *can* suspend me."

"I can suspend anybody I want."

"If you have a reason to suspend them, and I don't think you have a reason."

He gestured at the crowd all around us.

I looked at the crowd and noticed that

while most people were still dancing, some had pulled off their earbuds and were listening to us instead of music. Great, an audience.

"You know that I banned iPods, and I cancelled the school dance," he said.

"This isn't a school dance," I said. "This isn't school property, right?"

"No, it's not," he agreed.

"And as far as I can tell, we're free to leave school property at lunch. We're also free to use our iPods or cell phones or wear anything we want when we're not on school property. I'm not asking anybody to cut class. I just invited them to join me for lunch. I'm not doing anything wrong. At least nothing that could get me suspended." I paused. "Can I ask you a question?"

"Of course."

"You cancelled the school dance because there were behavior problems, right?"

"That was the reason."

"Fights, alcohol and bad behavior," I said.

"Those were the reasons."

"Look around. None of that happened here today." I gestured to Oswald who was still filming. "You can even look at the tape if you want. Just because something bad happened before doesn't mean it will happen again. Don't you think we deserve a chance?"

"I was willing to give you a chance, Ian. I thought you could be a real leader at this school," he said.

"That's what I'm trying to do," I said. "Isn't this leadership?" I asked, gesturing to the crowd. "And, if you let us have our dance, I'll try my best to make sure it happens the way it's supposed to happen."

Julia's suspension would be over by then. I'd ask her to help supervise. Maybe I'd even ask her if she wanted to come to the dance with...no, I wasn't ready for that—not yet. But there would be other dances.

Mr. Roberts didn't answer right away. He looked like he was thinking. That was a good thing.

"I'll make sure the dance works. You have my word on it," I said reassuringly, almost pleading.

Slowly he nodded his head. "I guess you really don't leave me much choice," Mr. Roberts said.

"You mean you'll let us have a dance?"

"We'll talk...after school. But, first things first."

He reached into his suit pocket and pulled out an iPod! He put the buds in his ears, pushed Play and started to dance.

Eric Walters is one of Canada's most successful writers for young readers with more than fifty novels to his credit. He is the only three-time winner of both the Silver Birch and the Red Maple Awards of the Ontario Library Association and has won numerous other children's choice awards. He tours across North America and has spoken to over a million children. For more information on Eric Walters, or to arrange a visit to your school, please visit www.ericwalters.net.